When the
Flame
Goes Out

DEBORAH NORTON

When the Flame Goes Out
by Deborah Norton
Based on a True Story

Printed in South Carolina, in the United States of America

Unless otherwise indicated, Bible quotations are taken from the *King James Version.* Public domain.

Cover Design by Narrow Way Design

ISBN-13: 978-1508951636
ISBN-10: 1508951632

DEDICATION

Lovingly dedicated to my lifelong, precious friend, Betty. Thank you for the memories.

ACKNOWLEDGMENTS

A huge thank you to Debbie Laws, Liz Davis, Barbara Gilstrap and my children; my biggest supporters! God bless you all, always!

PROLOGUE

Dakota had suffered an abusive childhood at the hands of her own mama. At the age of eleven the only person who believed in her and loved her enough to want to help came to her rescue. Mama Mary. Or as Dakota now called her, Mother.

Mother had been her guiding light. The speck of hope shattering the darkness surrounding Dakota, helping her through the trials of abuse. She was the rock in the sea of helplessness confronting her.

When Mother gained custody of Dakota, the child thought all of her worries were over. She knew she could not be loved more. Now it was 1986 and Dakota was grown. She was married with two small boys and her marriage was in trouble. Big Daddy died just three short months ago from a massive heart attack and now Mother was ill. Everything in Dakota's life was going wrong again. She needed her light...her flame in the dark. She needed Mother.

DEBORAH NORTON

CHAPTER ONE

Dakota paced the hallway in front of the fourth floor Intensive Care Unit inside St. Peter's hospital. She had been pacing for the past two weeks, barely eating and sleeping on the chairs in the waiting room. Mother was sick. The doctors said *very* sick. But Dakota had been visiting the chapel downstairs and praying faithfully every day and just knew Mother would be okay.

Her boys, Shane aged nine, and Adam aged six, were staying with their other Grandmother, 'Granny'. Dakota was not worried about them. She knew they were being well cared for. Her husband, George, had not even come to check on her. But she was not worried about him either. She was worried about Mother and how long she would have to stay in ICU.

She decided to go home just long enough to shower and change her clothes. Stepping to the information desk she spoke to the aid there. "Hi. I'm leaving for a short while. If you need me, I'll be at home. You have my number."

"Yes, Mrs. Day." The aid smiled and went back to her work.

Dakota wondered if George would be at home. She hoped not. They had argued so much lately. She wished he was still the boy she had fallen in love with in high school. *He was so sweet then,* she thought.

George was a couple of inches taller than Dakota's five-foot-seven frame. The thing that attracted her to him was his sea-blue eyes and the way he made her giggle. He was confident, smart, good-looking, and he seemed to love her unconditionally. Everyone said they made the perfect couple. His fair hair in contrast to her dark tresses and dark eyes. His gags and jokes in contrast to her seriousness. Opposites attract. Right?

For awhile, Dakota thought.

The children favored them. Shane looked like Dakota and Adam was the spitting image of George. They should have been the perfect family. The thought of how they really were made Dakota's stomach wrench into knots.

Pulling into the driveway she saw George's blue pickup parked next to the brick home they built last year. She went inside to find him pouring a cup of coffee. "Hi," she said.

"Well. About time you came home," he replied.

"I'm not staying", said Dakota. "I have to get back to the hospital. Mother is not any better."

"So why do you have to be there all the time? You're not a nurse. There's nothing you can do for her."

"I can be there for her," Dakota told him. "She has always been there for me." Inwardly, Dakota was seething. She always had to tip-toe around George.

"When are you going to be here for me, Dakota? When are you going to be here for the boys? You expect my mother to keep them all the time?"

Dakota let out a frustrated breath. "I know the boys need me, but your mother said she would be happy to keep them until Mother goes home. Please be patient. Just a little longer."

As Dakota headed for the bathroom to shower she wrapped her long dark hair in a towel, then heard George slinging dishes into the sink. "It's time for you to come home and *stay* home," he yelled.

It seems like the harder we try to make this marriage work the more it falls apart, Dakota thought. George and Dakota had been separated several times through the years. Many mistakes had been made. Many sins committed. But they always ended up back together to renew the love they had found as teenagers. *I can't think about that now. I'll deal with him later.*

The nurse was looking for Dakota when she returned to the hospital. "I'm afraid your mother has taken a turn for the worse," she said. "Is there another family member you could call to come sit with you?"

Dakota was stunned. Worse? Another family member? She stammered an answer. "Y-yes. I have a brother, Junior. I'll call him."

Mother and Big Daddy had adopted Junior when he was small. Dakota had been so jealous. Then she grew to love him as much as Mother and

Big Daddy. Before Dakota could get to the phone on the wall, Junior walked in.

His eighteen-year-old frame was tall and lean. A dimple in his chin could be seen even when he was not smiling and Dakota loved his quiet manner. His hazel eyes showed his concern as he hugged Dakota.

"How is she, Sis?"

"I'm worried, Junior. They just told me she is worse."

"Have they figured out why she's gotten worse?"

"The congestive heart failure has improved," Dakota told him, "but the diabetes is beginning to affect her kidneys and the doctor said he is seeing signs of Alzheimer's."

"It's time for our fifteen minute visit. Will they still let us go back?"

"The nurse asked that we wait a few minutes."

"Let's go to the chapel," Junior said.

The two held hands as they sat and prayed for Mother. Dakota began....

Father, we are here again to ask for your help. We thank you for all the blessings you have provided and we ask for one more. Please, Lord, please heal Mother. Let us take her back home soon. We need her in our lives so much. I need her as much as I have ever needed her. Please heal her quickly. Please let me see her the way she used to be, laughing, talking, happy to see us. In Jesus' name, Amen.

"Amen," Junior echoed. "Let's go check on her."

Mother remained the same for several more days. Junior had to return to work. Dakota continued to pace the floors and reminisced of how things used to be.

The nurse came out to the waiting room, interrupting her thoughts. "I have some pleasant news for you, Mrs. Day. Your mother is awake. A surprise for all of us!"

"May I see her?" Dakota was grinning from ear to ear.

"Yes, but just a few minutes. She needs her rest."

Dakota entered the cubicle quietly so as not to startle Mother. "Mother?"

"My Dakota," Mother responded. Slowly she opened her eyes.

Dakota bent down to plant a kiss on her forehead. "You have had us so worried," she said. "How are you feeling?"

"I have felt better," Mother replied. "But I would like to sit up for a while."

Dakota helped her to sit up and fluffed the pillow behind her. She then straightened the blankets and offered Mother a sip of water. "Feel like brushing your teeth?" Dakota asked.

Mother then went about brushing her teeth, washing her face and allowing Dakota to brush her graying hair. As Dakota pulled the brush through the thin strands, Mother asked about the grandchildren and Junior and told Dakota she was getting too thin. For several minutes Dakota saw Mother as she used to be. Smiling, talking, loving and being Mother. God had answered Dakota's prayer of seeing her that way once more. Then Mother began to tire. The nurse asked Dakota to leave so she could rest.

The next day the nurse sat down with Dakota. "Your mother is worse again. We are limiting visits to five minutes. It does not look good, Mrs. Day. You should call any family members who might want to see her."

Dakota could not believe what she was hearing. She entered the room and when she reached for Mother's hand recoiled and gasped. Mother's hand was completely black. "We think the IV backed up and her diabetes caused the blackness," the nurse told her. She is going downhill fast, Mrs. Day. But if she does survive this, I am sorry to tell you she will certainly lose her hand."

Dakota tried hard to hold the tears until she reached the chapel. Once there the river began. She fell to her knees between the pews and sobbed.

Father, I know you don't need my permission to take Mother home. I know that when it is time, she will go. I have been begging you to let her heal and to let her stay with us longer. But I know now that she could not survive the amputation of her hand. If you have let her stay this long for us, I thank you, Lord. I thank you for letting me see her one more time the way she used to be. I never thought I could say this, but she has suffered long enough, Father. She is ready to go home. Please take her quickly and put that beautiful smile back on her face. I know Daddy is ready to see her again. I don't know how I can face life without her, Lord. But I don't want her to hurt anymore.

Two hours later the nurse said it was time. Dakota had the aid call Junior to the hospital, but he had not yet arrived. The nurse asked Dakota if she would like to go back to be with Mother when she made her passage into heaven. Dakota was crying so hard she could barely speak.

"I can't. *I can't!* God answered my prayer in letting me see her the way she used to be earlier. That is how I want to remember her. *I can't watch her die!*"

Two of Mother's nieces were there. They said they would keep Mother company. By the time Junior arrived, Mother had passed. Everyone embraced and cried quietly. The nurse tried to console Dakota by telling her that Mother was asleep when she passed and left peacefully. "She loved God," she reminded Dakota. "She is with the angels now." But Dakota was inconsolable.

The following day Dakota and Junior knew what had to be done. Arrangements had to be made. They had just gone through this with Big Daddy. Somehow, Dakota fumbled her way through the day. She was numb. The tears had stopped and shock took their place. That night, she tried to sleep. Sleep had always been her escape, but somehow sleep would not come now. Dozing for a few minutes here and there the night passed slowly.

Neighbors began to show up at her house. Food was piled high on the kitchen counters, but Dakota could not bring herself to eat. She was like a robot with no human qualities. She couldn't eat, couldn't sleep, couldn't cry and did not want to talk. George didn't bother her and helped his mother take care of the children.

Visitation and viewing was scheduled for seven o'clock in the evening. The line of people was out the church door. Junior and Dakota were both exhausted but they knew Mother would want them to do the right thing and embrace every single visitor. So they did.

It was almost ten o'clock when they all went home and again sleep would not come. At midnight Dakota was sitting in the great room in the dark staring out the French doors into the back yard at nothing in particular. George came into the room with a glass.

"Drink this," he told her. "Drink it down." She didn't ask what it was but simply did as she was told. It smelled of whiskey and burned as it went down. Soon she was asleep and spent the night on the couch.

Granny still had the boys so George and Dakota drove to the church alone. "Would you stop at the florist, please? I'd like to get two long-stemmed red roses. One for me and one for Junior."

Dakota didn't hear a single word at the service. Her thoughts ran rampant. Her memories going back in time to when she was a little girl and the times she stayed with Mother as her foster child. Oh how she missed the times with Mother at church. She loved the people there and she loved being there so much. Now, even if she attended the same church it would never be the same.

Then Dakota's thoughts went back even further to a time she could not remember, but had been told of. When Dakota was still a tiny baby her Mama had given her away. The people she had been given to was Mother and Big Daddy.

Since Mother and Big Daddy could not have children of their own they were thrilled to get Dakota. For four years they loved her. They dressed her like a tiny princess and showed her off to everyone they met. Then came that day when two women showed up at her Sunday School class and asked for Dakota. "Can Dakota come with us?" The Sunday School teacher had seen the women in church and Dakota went to them readily so she let Dakota go. No one knew the women were there to kidnap Dakota. No one knew they were taking Dakota back to her birth mother.

"Where is she?" Mother panicked. The church was searched over and over but no one could find Mother and Big Daddy's little girl. Nothing could be done. The police reported back to them that Dakota was safe and in the care of her Mama. Dakota had been given away, but no papers were signed. An adoption had not taken place so there was nothing they could do to get Dakota back.

Mother and Big Daddy sat in their white rocking chairs on the front porch and cried for days on end. Then they determined to keep loving Dakota and spend time with her when they could. So they went to see Dakota and her Mama and vowed to stay in touch. Dakota had known all of her life that she loved them. But she could not remember the early days when that bond had been formed.

Now she was at the cemetery, but again she did not hear a word. She simply stared at the casket wanting it all to be a bad dream. George nudged her forward and she laid the single rose on top of the casket and turned to head for the mortuary's family car. Junior did the same. That is when she realized that Mother would be lowered into the earth and it would be the last time she gave Mother roses. It was also when she realized she could not breathe.

The driver of the car saw that she was hyperventilating and shoved a brown paper bag at George. He helped her to sit down on the back seat and put the bag over her mouth. "Breathe deep," he told her.

Precious in the sight of the LORD is the death of his saints. Psalm 116:15

CHAPTER TWO

I never knew the death of a loved one could hurt so bad physically! Dakota held her stomach tightly. She had hurt when Big Daddy died but this was beyond pain. Her stomach heaved, her heart raced. She fought to breathe and tears were non-stop. George slid onto the seat beside her and asked the driver to take them to their car. By the time they arrived back at the church Dakota had at least settled enough to breathe again. "You okay, now?" George helped her into their car.

"I'm okay." But she wasn't okay. *I will never be okay,* she thought.

As soon as Dakota got home she went to the cabinet where George kept a bottle of Brandy. She poured a shot glass full and downed the warm beverage. "Whoa, whoa, whoa!" George warned her. "You're not used to that stuff. Take it easy."

"Is this what you gave me to help me sleep?"

George reached for the bottle. "Yes."

"Then this is what I need." Dakota pulled the liquor back before he could take it. She then poured another shot and downed it quickly.

"You are going to drink yourself into a stupor," George said.

"Exactly!" Dakota swaddled the bottle and took it with her to the patio. George followed her and began his rant. "You are not the first person to lose someone, Dakota. You are acting like it is the end of the world. You don't need to drink yourself to sleep."

Dakota was beginning to feel the effects of the Brandy. The alcohol gave her courage she did not normally have where George was concerned. Looking at him through squinted eyes she returned a rant of her own.

"How dare you? How dare you tell me how to mourn my mother? No, I am not the first person to lose someone, but this is the first time *I* have lost someone that meant this much to me! So, yes. It is very much like the end of the world! The end of *my* world as I know it! It's a crying shame you don't know how to love someone that much!" Dakota then threw the shot glass at the brick barbecue pit and turned the bottle up. Settling into an oversized wicker chair she cradled the bottle like a baby and sat staring at George. Daring him to respond.

"Suit yourself," he said. He went inside leaving her with her sorrow.

For several days Dakota did nothing but sit and stare. Her mother-in-law was understanding; George was not. He had long run out of patience and stayed on Dakota about bringing the children back home.

Eventually she did. But Dakota had a secret. Dakota had developed a liking for alcohol.

George worked from three o'clock until eleven o'clock in the evenings. After the boys were in bed Dakota drank herself to sleep. It was a dangerous thing to do, but she was not thinking straight. She was not thinking at all. She was desperately trying to numb her pain. Part of her pain was George.

George was not a sociable man. He did not want to go anywhere to visit. He did not want visitors. He did not want Dakota working or socializing or having friends. He wanted all of his life to be kept inside the house that Dakota was beginning to hate. He was not the husband Dakota longed for. He was more of a king over his kingdom.

One afternoon Dakota threw the empty brandy bottle into the trash. Going through the cabinets she was frustrated to find there was no more. *Oh great!* she thought. The wheels began to turn. She knew George liked a drink once in awhile, but she also knew he would not get her more liquor, so she went to the neighbors house. Knock, knock, knock. With the boys in tow she hoped Beatrice was home.

"Beatrice! I am so glad you are here. I wonder if you would mind watching the boys for just a few minutes? I need to run an errand."

"Sure," Beatrice responded.

"I shouldn't be long," Dakota told her.

There wasn't much gas in the Chrysler. George never put more than a couple of dollars at a time in it. He didn't want her going anywhere. Dakota hoped it would get her to a small nearby town. A plan was forming in her mind. George knew where every cent of his money went. Dakota never went shopping alone. Either he or his mother was always with her. George did not like for her to go anywhere alone. She would have to be careful with her spending or he would be furious! Not because she was buying liquor, but because she went out alone and didn't tell him.

I'll go into the grocery store and buy some hamburger meat. That's what I'll cook for supper. That's a good reason for going to the store. I'll write a check and make it out for more than the meat cost. That way I'll get some money back for the liquor and a couple of dollars for gas. If he finds out I'll just have to live with him yelling at me for the next week! That is what I'll do every time I buy groceries. I'll cut back on my diet drinks and get cash back for gas and brandy.

Somehow she got away with it! The bottle lasted until the next trip to the grocery store. This time Dakota called her mother-in-law. George didn't mind if Dakota went to see his mother. George's mother didn't drive. She was happy for Dakota to suggest she take her shopping. George's mother also liked to go to the liquor store. So Dakota told her, "Sit still and let me go in to get your purchases." Dakota was able to get her own and when she returned to the car she carefully hid it in the trunk.

Dakota knew what she was doing was wrong. She felt guilty about it until the warm liquid hit her veins. Then there was no guilt. Only anger. Angry she had let herself get into a verbally abusive relationship. A marriage where her mind was controlled, every movement was manipulated and love was non-existent. Had she not had enough of that as a child? She was also angry she let herself become dependent on liquid comfort, and most of all angry at God for taking her mother.

One night George came home from work early. Normally Dakota was asleep by the time he got home, but tonight she was awake and tipsy.

"Is that brandy I smell?"

"Yes it is." She was defiant. She waited for the explosion. She didn't have to wait long.

"Have you lost your mind, Dakota? You're drinking on the sly by yourself? Where are the boys?"

"They are asleep," she told him. Dakota tried to leave the room to escape his criticism but it was no use. He followed her every step finding it hard to keep his voice down so as not to wake the children.

"Leave me alone," she said.

"No! I won't leave you alone. You will do what I tell you and I am telling you to leave the brandy alone!

"You were the one that got me started on brandy. Now you're yelling at me about it? Leave. Me. Alone!"

"Dakota, what would your mother say about you drinking?"

"You leave my mother out of this. Besides, she can't say anything about it. I am a grown woman. I will drink if I want to."

"Not on my dime, you won't."

"Then I will get a job! All you care about is your precious money."

"You will not get a job and you are drunk."

"Not yet, I'm not."

Day after day, week after week the arguments continued. The more they argued the more Dakota turned inward. The more she turned inward, the more she drank. George threatened to find comfort with another woman, but by now Dakota didn't even care. *He has already committed adultery in his heart anyway,* she thought.

Soon she learned the secret of hiding the smell of the liquor by drinking vodka and that seemed to calm the storm a little. She also learned how to get through each day just shy of being drunk. She cooked and cleaned and cared for the boys all the while numbing the pain of Mother's death and her disintegrating marriage.

Dakota began to go for walks after the children left for school. Since George worked late he usually slept late so she would take her first drink of the day with her orange juice and go exploring.

A short distance from home was a dilapidated old church building. The roof was gone, the walls crumbling. There was an archway where the door once stood. The stained glass lay in shards below the long, tall windows. Dakota approached the building with disdain. There was a time when she would have felt nothing but revered respect for such a place. Now she almost sneered at it and kept walking. She saw the sign hanging from one chain. *Country Chapel,* it read. *Ha!* Dakota thought. *More like Forgotten Chapel.* For a brief moment Dakota remembered how she had memorized the whole book of Philippians from the Bible as a child and had a fleeting yearning to read it again. Then she remembered. She was mad at God and she needed another drink.

That night Dakota tossed and turned in fitful sleep. When Dakota was a child there was a recurring dream that haunted her sleep for years.

That haunting returned now in her alcohol induced slumber.

The nightmare was always the same. Something was after Dakota. She couldn't see what it was but she knew she was in danger. She ran from the peril through a maze of hallways and they all looked identical. It was like looking down a hall with tunnel vision and each hallway was mirrored, sterile, clean. They brought to mind a hospital yet no one could be seen. The space surrounding Dakota was dark, but the hallway ahead of her was brightly lit. As she ran the halls she tried to escape the menacing dark circle by running into the brightly lit areas, but the darkness kept up with her.

Dakota was terrified. The danger was catching up to her. It was hard to breathe now. She was tiring from running hallway after hallway. Finally she darted into a room and found a heavy gray desk. She pulled the chair out from under the desk and crawled into the cubby, pulling the chair back in to hide her. Gasping for air, Dakota froze with fear when she heard a voice calling her name just outside of her hiding place.

"Dakota," it whispered wickedly.

Dakota squeezed her eyes tight. *Please go away, please go away!* As tightly as she closed her eyes the tears still found their way out.

"Dakota! Dakota, wake up!" George was shaking her, waking her from the nightmare. As a child, Mother always came to her rescue in the dream. Now George woke her before Mother arrived.

"What?" she asked. "Why are you waking me up?"

"You were having a nightmare," George responded.

"If you had left me alone I would have seen Mother. She always saved me when I had this dream."

"Next time I'll be sure to ask." George rolled over and went back to sleep.

Woe unto them that rise up early in the morning, [that] they may follow strong drink; that continue until night, [till] wine inflame them! Isaiah 5:11

CHAPTER THREE

Dakota was lonely. She missed talking to Mother on the phone. It was difficult to talk to George anymore and he made it impossible to have friends. He wanted her all to himself and it wasn't worth the constant fight and the hell she would live through to try to have a friend. Then Dakota remembered Joyce. Joyce had been a lifelong friend at the church Mother took her to as a child. She had seen her at Mother's funeral and Joyce asked Dakota to call her sometime.

After George left for work she decided to call. "Hi, Joyce. It's Dakota. How are you?"

"Dakota! Oh my goodness! It sure is good to hear from you. I was worried about you at the funeral. You looked so pale."

Dakota was immediately at ease. She had always loved this lady and now she had someone to talk to. So she began calling her a couple of times a week. Soon she began confiding in her about her failing marriage and mentioned she had thought about separating from George.

The next day George kept staring at her over the lunch table. Finally he asked her, "So you want us to separate do you?"

Dakota looked at George through narrowed eyes. Thoughts ran rampart as she tried to comprehend what he had said. Joyce was the only person she had mentioned separation to and her friend would not have betrayed her. So how did he know?

Falteringly, she responded. "It has crossed my mind," she said. "How did you know?"

"I hear things," he replied. "I also hear your girlfriend thinks you should pack your bags even if you do not file for legal separation. Who does she think she is?"

That afternoon Dakota called Joyce again. She told her about George mentioning separation. "I didn't tell *anybody*" the woman said. "Do you think he is recording your phone conversations?"

"I don't know. Let's hang up now."

Dakota began looking under the night stand and all around the phone in the bedroom. This was the phone she had called from. Then it occurred to her she should check under the floor where the phone line came from.

Quickly she headed to the basement. The cement block basement was the length of the house and was used mainly for storage and a place for the kids to play. She tried to guess about where the night stand was as she looked up at the unfinished ceiling. Then she saw it. A bunch of colored wires that had been spliced together and wrapped with electrical tape right next to a small metal box. He *was* recording her phone calls! Now Dakota was furious and scared. If he would do this what else would he do? She needed to leave. She needed a plan. But first she needed a drink.

Sunday morning found Dakota with a pounding headache. As she poured coffee into her favorite cup she decided she would ask about taking the boys to church. "Think there's enough gas in the car to take Shane and Adam to church this morning?"

"I thought you were mad at God," he retorted.

"Yes, and mad at the preacher too. Beatrice told him that Mother died and he has not visited or called. But me being mad should not take away the children's privilege of going to church. Of course you could take them."

"No, thanks." George gave her a puzzled look. "Yes, there is a little gas in the car. You can take them."

Dakota sat on a pew in the back of the sanctuary. After a couple of hymns the pastor asked if anyone needed prayer. Dakota was surprised to see blond-haired Adam raise his hand. When the pastor asked him what he needed prayer for the six year-old pointed at Dakota, his puppy-dog brown eyes saddened. "My Mommy has a headache," he said.

The pastor smiled and stepped over to Dakota. "May I pray for you?" He asked.

"Of course," she replied and smiled at her thoughtful son.

Dakota didn't pray. She simply stood still and let the preacher pray for her.

After church, Dakota cooked the normal Sunday fare: fried chicken and vegetables. As they sat to eat,

Adam asked, "Mommy, does your head feel better since the preacher laid his hands on you and prayed?"

George jerked his head around sharply to look at Dakota. "What does he mean he laid his hands on you?"

"It's in the Bible, George. Believers lay their hands on those who are sick and pray for them."

"That's it!" George was furious. He slammed his fork down on the table. "Nobody is going to put his hands on you! That is the *last time* you will go to church!"

Dakota was dumbfounded. Staring at him it was like a light bulb went off in her head. She could see so clearly now. She thought of George's subtle changes over the years to control and dominate. No friends, very little time with family, and now he was saying no church! If she was unsure before, she was absolutely sure now. Even if she *was* mad at God, this was the United States of America and no one could take away her privilege of going to church. God would not want her to live this way.

Dakota had learned a long time ago that arguing with George was futile. No one won an argument in this house but him. She didn't want to get the boys upset so she simply sat down and began passing the food around the table. She tried to hide the fact that she was flabbergasted.

Dakota's childhood had been filled with abuse. Both verbal and physical. This was different yet it felt the same. She had succeeded in getting away from the abuse as a child by running away time after time after time until finally someone heard her silent plea for help. But now she had two small children.

Somehow it changed how she would have to handle things and she didn't know where to start. Dakota wasn't hungry anymore. She needed a drink.

Now that Dakota knew George was recording her phone conversations she only spoke with her mother-in-law on the phone. She did not call Joyce anymore and Joyce understood why but Dakota missed talking to her. She needed some advice but dared not call from the house phone. The children were at school and George had gone into work early so Dakota went to the grocery store and the liquor store and after making her purchases used the pay phone just outside of the building.

"Hello?"

"Hey, Joyce. It's Dakota."

"Dakota....are you at home?"

"No, I ran an errand and I'm using a pay phone."

"Good," Joyce said. "Are you okay? I've been thinking about you."

"I'm doing okay," Dakota replied. "You were right. George has been recording everything on the phone. I don't know what to do, Joyce. I know I don't want to be with George anymore. He has killed all the love I ever had for him and I feel like there are invisible bars on all the windows. He has said I can never go to church again, but how can I leave? I have no money. I don't have a job, but I do have two small children that need us both."

"You need to talk to a lawyer, Dakota."

"I don't know any lawyers," Dakota said.

"Look in the phone book. Look for one who specializes in families. But only if you are sure. God doesn't like divorce. Only if adultery is involved."

"Oh I am sure alright! Adultery is a possibility on both sides if things stay the way they are. Even if we don't divorce it is becoming impossible to stay. I will write down some numbers and call from here later," she told her. "I will let you know when I find one."

Dakota set an appointment for a consultation with a divorce lawyer for later that week. His name was W.R. Barr and she was a shipwreck by the time she got there. The lawyer told her before she could file for divorce she first had to file for legal separation. When she told him she had not left George yet she was shocked to hear him say, "That's okay. You can be separated and still live under the same roof. Of course you will want to find other living arrangements eventually if he refuses to leave the house."

"You don't understand, Mr. Barr. It is almost impossible to live there now. How am I going to stay there while separated from him?"`

"Usually people who do this have no other choice. They have nowhere to go. So they sleep on the couch and spend a lot of time away from home until they can make their own way. Legal separation is the only way we can get you temporary financial help once you are on your own."

Dakota took a deep breath. "Okay," she said. "File for separation."

Dakota left the building in a state of numbness. She couldn't think. She sat in her car for fifteen minutes just staring at the steering wheel. *I did it! I can't believe I just filed for separation! It is not going to be easy staying in that house!*

That night proved her thoughts right. George was furious. He could not believe what he was hearing. "You did *what?"*

"I filed for legal separation."

"Have you lost your mind? We can't separate. I am not leaving this house. I built it with my own hands! We have two children. How are you going to support yourself?" He was rambling. Searching for a way to keep her.

Dakota had made a pot of coffee and was pouring for the both of them. They sat down at the kitchen table and Dakota sipped the hot liquid while George carried on. Dakota yearned for the vodka but knew this was one time she had to fight sober.

"Well say *something* for Pete's sake!" George stared at her, waiting.

"Don't you think we have said everything there is to say, George? Haven't we hashed it all out, over and over again? I am not happy. You are not happy. We could stay together, but all it is going to do is make the boys unhappy too."

"The boys are fine," George quipped.

Dakota used both hands to push her hair back from her face. She was frustrated and needed to do something besides sit here arguing with George. She hated confrontation of any kind and the butterflies were giving her stomach havoc.

"For tonight let's not argue anymore," she said. "You have just gotten the news. Let it sink in." Dakota stood and began toward the bedroom to get a pillow and blanket. "I will sleep out here on the couch."

George stood and left the house slamming the door behind him. Dakota was surprised to see Shane stumble sleepily into the kitchen. "Where is Daddy going, Mama?"

"Probably to see his mother," she replied. Something she wished *she* could do.

Likewise, ye husbands, dwell with them according to knowledge, giving honour unto the wife, as unto the weaker vessel, and as being heirs together of the grace of life; that your prayers be not hindered. 1 Peter 3:7

CHAPTER FOUR

The next several weeks were hard for both George and Dakota. When they were alone in the house they didn't even speak. When the children were present they put up a façade of pretending to care. The one thing they agreed on was keeping as much of the heartbreak from the children as they could.

Dakota went to the bank and withdrew enough money to get her through until she could find work. Of course George yelled at her but she was used to that. She still sneaked in the vodka but had cut back on it's intake. She had applied for a position at a local restaurant. Cooking and cleaning was pretty much all she knew how to do. She waited on pins and needles for an answer as to whether she had the job.

One night Dakota decided she couldn't stand to stay in the house until George went to bed. It was a Sunday evening and the children had just finished dinner. Junior was out on a date and she had no place to go. She thought about going to visit Joyce, but she lived so far away Dakota decided against it. She was still mad at the preacher and still mad at God, but she felt she would fare better at the all night prayer service than she would sitting in the den staring at whatever TV show George decided to watch.

"I am going to church tonight," she said to Shane in front of George. "Tell Adam it is time to get ready for bed." Shane left the room.

"Church?" George exclaimed. "This late on a Sunday night? Ha! Sure you are!"

"Yes, George. It is an all night prayer meeting."

"What kind of excuse will you come up with next Sunday night? You say you are mad at God, yet you are going to pray?"

"What are you insinuating, George?"

"Why don't you just say you are going to meet somebody, Dakota?"

"Because I am not going to meet somebody and I definitely can't sit here!"

She went to tuck the boys into bed, changed her blouse, then met George in the kitchen on her way out. He blocked the door. "Excuse me," she said.

George placed two fingers on her chest pushing them into her forcefully, causing her to take a step backwards with every word he said.

"I had better not hear of you out with another man!"

Dakota's eyes filled with tears. George had never failed to be verbally abusive, but he had never physically pushed her and now she was sure if he was agitated to a point, he was capable of hurting her. Rather than irritate him more she simply answered his accusation with, "You won't!" He then let her pass and she quickly went to her car in the garage.

When Dakota arrived at the church the prayer meeting had already begun. She quietly slipped into the back pew. *Good,* she thought. *No one saw me come in.* Her intentions were to sit peacefully until she was sure George had gone to bed. After about an hour she noticed the preacher stand up and reach for a pitcher of water. He looked at her but did not acknowledge her and went back to his prayers. Dakota sat for another hour listening to the whispering sounds of the prayers of the others and decided she wanted to leave.

The parking lot was not full and it was easy to remember where she had parked. As she started her car she backed out of the parking space and as she did she noticed in her rear view mirror the headlights on another vehicle come on.

Well that's weird, she thought. *That car is not in the parking lot. It is on the side of the road and no one else has left the church. That is really strange.* Dakota decided to wait a minute to see if she could see what kind of vehicle it was in case someone had been stealing from cars in the parking lot. But the car did not move. So Dakota pulled up to the exit drive and as she pulled onto the road the car fell in behind her. It was dark and Dakota could not tell anything about the car or the person in it. Then when she turned at the next left she noticed the other car did too. *Hmmm. Is that car following me?*

Dakota decided to see if the car was indeed following her. She slowed and made a U turn in the middle of the country road. Watching in her rear view mirror she noticed the car behind her did the same. Dakota headed for the nearest town. She locked her doors and slowed down to a crawl. The car had plenty of opportunity to pass on the dark highway, but didn't. So Dakota sped up. As she did, the car following her sped up too. Then it occurred to her that George had probably sent someone to follow her.

Well he isn't the brightest bulb in the box, she thought. *Probably thinks he is doing such a good job. Well, let's just see how smart he is and give him a run for his money!*

Dakota floored the gas pedal at the edge of town leaving the car temporarily in her dust. She didn't even slow down when she approached a blind curve. Speeding just past the curve she quickly pulled into a gas station hiding behind two gas pumps. She watched as the car following her sped past the gas station, it's driver thinking she had continued into town. She then pulled back into the road and drove in the opposite direction to the nearest fast food restaurant. She parked her car in a dark area and went inside. She ordered a coffee and sat down to think about what had just taken place. *This is unbelievable,* she thought. *First he records my phone conversations and now he puts a tail on me! What is next? I need to go home, but I dread it so much. George is probably laughing and feeling pretty smug right now. I need a drink.*

Dakota began her drive home slowly. She didn't see anyone behind her all the way and wondered if she would have to face George tonight. She was almost home when she saw the old forgotten chapel. On the spur of the moment she decided to turn into an opening next to it. *This was probably where the driveway used to be,* she thought. *I will park the car here for tonight and maybe George won't hear me coming home.*

Dakota reached for the flashlight in the door pocket and walked the short distance home. She sneaked into the house and went to the basement to don her nightgown. Just as she settled onto the couch, George flipped the light switch on. "Where have you been?" he shouted.

"George, hold your voice down! Can't we talk about this tomorrow?"

"No, we will talk about this now."

"Fine," Dakota answered him. "I have been at church."

"I am talking about after church," he said.

"Who said I went somewhere after church?" She looked at him accusingly.

George turned the light switch off and went back to the bedroom. *Good,* thought Dakota. *Maybe now I can get some sleep.*

Just as she thought that the bedroom door opened again. George was not done. "I guess you think you are smart outrunning my friend tonight."

"It crossed my mind," she retorted.

"You won't lose him again." With that George turned the light off and again headed for the bedroom.

Quickly, before he could come back out for another rant, Dakota grabbed her throw and her flashlight and slipped out the door. She didn't even care she had only her nightgown on. The neighbors were far and few. She gingerly made her way back to where her car was parked at the chapel silently wishing she had grabbed her shoes. When she reached her car she went to the trunk to find her bottle of vodka. She had become so accustomed to the taste that she didn't even need a chaser or a mixer anymore. She drank and cursed and cursed and drank. As she sat in her car whining about how unfair life was, she became more drunk than she had ever been.

The clouds parted to reveal a Strawberry Moon shining into the old church. Leaving the car she found her way to the ruins of the building. The crumbled brick and cement didn't slow her as she ascended the broken steps.

"God? You home?" Dakota yelled in her drunken stupor. She stumbled as she moved into the ruins. "I think we need to talk," she said. "I have some questions."

A large chunk of a wall was near the door on the floor. Dakota teetered toward it and losing her balance sat down on it hard. "Whew, almost lost my bottle!" she declared. She turned the decanter up, emptying it's contents, and tossed the bottle adding to the debris behind her.

Her speech was loud, slow and slurred. "Now, about that talk. I know we haven't talked in a long time, God, but I have been sad and mad and hurt and....well....why?" She shrugged her shoulders and threw up her hands. "Just tell me why. Is this your plan for my life God? 'Cause if it is I need to ask you to change it."

Dakota stood to climb onto the chunk of wall. "Do I need to get closer for you to hear me, God? You said you had a plan for me," she yelled. "At least that's what Mother said. Is this your plan? A plan for a mama that hated me? A plan to take away the mother who loved me? A plan for me to be miserable in my marriage and now a God that won't talk to me?"

Dakota knew if she were sober she would never have talked to God that way. She began to feel guilty and to weep.

I guess He will punish me big time now. I have never spoken to anyone like this. Why do I not care now? If God just knocked me down dead right now I just wouldn't care.

She stumbled her way back to the car. Covering herself with the throw she had brought with her, she spent the rest of the night in the backseat as the vodka caused her to sleep.

Morning sun woke Dakota. That and the sound of the school bus riding by. "Oh, no!" she whispered.

O LORD, how long shall I cry, and thou wilt not hear! even cry out unto thee of violence, and thou wilt not save! Habakkuk 1:2

CHAPTER FIVE

Dakota sat up and her head began to throb about the time she remembered why she was sleeping in her car. *I hope George got the boys ready in time for the bus.*

Dakota slipped into the quiet house and peeked into the boys room to see they were still asleep. She woke them quickly and went into the kitchen to set out cereal bowls, then went to the basement to throw on some jeans and a t-shirt. Somehow she managed to get them to school on time without waking George.

Later that morning George came into the kitchen for coffee. "It must have been late when you came in the second time," George said.

Oh, please don't badger me this morning, Dakota thought.

She didn't want to be here, but needed to stay by the phone. She was hoping word would come today about a job she had applied for.

"Where were you?" he asked.

Here we go!

Dakota's headache intensified and now she didn't feel well at all. Slightly nauseated she stood to go to the bathroom. *Whoa!* She sat back down with a whump. She felt hot yet a cold chill ran over her. She was finding it hard to breathe and wiped her forehead with a napkin in an attempt to wipe away the clamminess. Somehow she made her way into the bedroom. She had not been in here for days but she needed to lie down. She opened the window next to the bed and struggled to gulp in the cool air.

Now her heart rate began to change. Thump, thump, thump. Rapidly the hard thumps increased until her heart rate was over one hundred seventy beats per minute. Dakota grimaced with pain.

"What are you doing?" asked George. He stood at the doorway frowning. "It's the middle of the morning. You can't sleep in the middle of the day!"

"I feel like....I am....having a heart attack." Dakota struggled to get the words out. "I feel like I am dying." Tears began to slide down Dakota's face. She was scared. She felt like her heart was coming out of her chest.

George walked over to where she lay and put his hand on her forehead. He looked at her closely and said , "You are not having a heart attack. You will be fine." Closing the open window, he then left the room pulling the door closed behind him.

After an hour Dakota's heart rate slowed and, feeling like she had run a marathon, she fell into a restless sleep for most of the day. When she awoke her chest was sore and she was still tired. She was shocked that she had slept so long. George was in the backyard with the children. She could hear their shrieks of playful laughter and she dreaded telling them they would soon be living somewhere else. Knowing the kids were okay she pulled a blanket up over her head. *I don't ever want to get back out of this bed,* she thought.

A root of bitterness had been planted. Depression set in deep. For several more days the 'heart episodes' continued and Dakota was convinced she was having mild heart attacks. Just as bad as having these attacks, she was furious that George didn't care that she could be dying. Eventually Dakota drove to the doctor's office alone.

Test after test was run. Blood samples were taken. The doctor did a full examination and told Dakota to come to his private office after she was dressed.

"Well," the doctor said, "it looks like your husband was right. These episodes you are having are not heart attacks. They are anxiety attacks or, as some call them, panic attacks."

Dakota took in a breath of relief. Then she addressed the doctor. "They sure felt like I was dying," she told him. "So now what?"

"Now you get rid of all the stress in your life," he said.

Dakota laughed out loud. "Okay," she replied. "First I will divorce my husband, then I will jerk the phone off the wall, then I will bring you two precious little boys that you can adopt, then I will find that job I need and that should just about take care of the stress."

The doctor looked at her long and hard. "You've had a major life change with the death of both parents. That takes some getting used to. Besides the attacks you are having, you are also suffering from depression. You are on the verge of tears right now. I am going to prescribe some anti-depressants and suggest you get some rest."

Rest. Yeah, that is just what I need. I need to sleep straight through a whole year.

Dakota stopped at the pharmacy on the way home to get her prescriptions filled. She was shocked at how much the doctor had prescribed.

"Oh my!" she told the pharmacist. "This is a lot, isn't it?" Dakota looked at the three bottles of pills.

"It's a little more than usual," he said. "Xanax, Valium and Vivactil are all strong medications. Be sure to follow the label directions closely and stay away from alcohol while you are taking these."

Are you kidding? Alcohol is the only thing that has gotten me through the last few weeks! Then Dakota stopped at the liquor store on the way home.

It was early and George had not left for work but Dakota needed to go home because the children would be getting off the bus. *I'll just stop at the old abandoned church until he leaves,* she thought.

As she sat in the car staring at the ruins of the building and sipping her spirits, she thought what a shame that time and neglect had destroyed it. "Looks like you and I have met the same fate." She had spoken out loud and toasted the shabby remnants of what was once beautiful.

As she spoke she looked through the broken openings and noticed the top of a tombstone behind the church. *Hmmm,* she thought, *I've never noticed that before.* She put the bottle of vodka back in the trunk and carefully made her way through the brambles to the back side of the church. She walked among the graves in the unkempt cemetery and stopped at one that caught her eye.

Wife, Mother, Friend. The monument had an angel atop and Dakota immediately remembered words Mother had spoken to her as a child. "Remember, Dakota. God's angels will always be watching over you."

Guess that was true only as long as she was here praying for me. This angel has seen better days, she thought. The angel had large wings and one of them was broken. Green algae covered most of it and the face was stern. Not even a half smile. *Too bad they are not still watching.* Then she sat at the foot of the unknown mother's grave and cried.

The sound of the school bus brought her back to the realization that she needed to go home. She made her way back to the car and went home to take care of the boys. Just as she pulled into the driveway the bus stopped to let them off. The driveway was long so she stopped to let the boys ride up to the house. A teenage girl stepped off the bus with them.

"Mrs. Day?" Dakota rolled the window down. "Yes?"

"Mrs. Day, my name is Teresa. I just wanted to let you know that sometimes the bigger kids pick on the little kids on the bus, so I put Adam on my lap every day to keep them away from him." Teresa was a beautiful, slim, tall, mature seventeen-year-old with skin the color of molasses.

"Well thank you, honey. What did you say your name is?"

"Teresa, Ma'am"

"Teresa, are you sure you are not an angel watching over my son?"

"Ma'am?"

"Never mind. Thank you."

As soon as they got inside the house Dakota heard the phone ringing. She ran to answer it breathless. "Hello?"

"Hello, may I speak with Dakota Day, please?"

"This is Dakota."

"Mrs. Day, I am calling about a job application you filled out."

"Yes," Dakota said. "I have been expecting your call. Is this Mrs. Sheeler?"

"Yes it is. When can you start work?"

"Is tomorrow too soon?" Dakota asked.

"Tomorrow is fine. You will be in a six week training program."

"Six weeks? To be a cashier?"

"Oh no." Mrs. Sheeler laughed. "You are a perfect candidate for our management team. Be here at nine o'clock in the morning."

For he shall give his angels charge over thee, to keep thee in all thy ways. Psalm 91:11

CHAPTER SIX

Dakota was going to work. She was nervous. It was just a fast food burger joint but she didn't know what to expect. Especially training for management. That part of her new job came as a surprise to her. It had been years since she had worked and even then it had been as a cashier in a grocery store.

Dakota liked Mrs. Sheeler immediately and found herself telling her all about her situation in hopes that the woman would work with her on a schedule around the boys' school schedule. To Dakota's surprise and relief Mrs. Sheeler said she would.

Finally! A job. Now I can start planning to move.

Dakota worked hard at her new job. As soon as the boys left for school she got ready and went to work. Then she got home in the afternoons just before they did. It was all working out well. Dakota missed her orange juice and liquor in the mornings but continued to drink at night.

She was amazed how fast she made friends with fellow employees and customers alike. It was something she needed in her life, now more than ever.

She was also glad that her new schedule allowed that the only time she saw George was on the weekends. After training she would have to work some on weekends but knew that George or his mother would take care of Shane and Adam. Junior was young and just beginning his life so she didn't ask him to baby sit.

After working for three weeks Dakota began looking for a place to live. She had become friends with a girl at work named Phyllis and told her what she was looking for.

"I know someone who has exactly what you need," Phyllis said. "I will write down her number and you can call her and ask about it. Dakota called the number Phyllis gave her.

"Hello, Mrs. Stone?"

"Yes."

"Mrs. Stone, my name is Dakota Day. A friend named Phyllis gave me your number. She said you have rental property. Is it still available?"

"Yes it is," the woman said. "Would you like to see it?"

"Yes!"

Dakota set up a time for Saturday to check out the house. She called her mother-in-law to ask her to watch the boys. The call was a little awkward because George's mother was upset at Dakota for leaving George. But she loved having the kids and she loved Dakota so she agreed.

Saturday came and the children were excited to be going to Granny's. Dakota dressed in jeans and a blue flannel shirt. She had lost a lot of weight and the clothes hung loose. *Well, at least I'm comfortable,* she thought.

Dakota had never done any kind of business dealings so she was nervous about today. She was still depressed and still had the occasional panic attack but because she was now working in the public, she had learned to fake a smile throughout the day. The medicines the doctor had prescribed for her were too strong to take while working. She took them when she was not working but she felt like a zombie and if she took a drink with them they put her out like a light.

Dakota didn't like how she felt with the medicine but she also didn't like how she felt without the medicine. Even so she knew she had to be strong for the boys, so she faked her way through each day hoping an attack did not come at work.

When Dakota arrived at the address Mrs. Stone had given her, Mrs. Stone was already there. "Hi!" Dakota greeted the older woman.

"Good morning," she replied. "Before we take the grand tour, I have a few questions to ask."

"Okay," said Dakota.

Mrs. Stone led her to a bench in the yard under a big shade tree. Dakota looked around as they settled and knew already she loved the place. Mrs. Stone asked her some questions about her job and pets and children. Dakota answered them all to the woman's satisfaction and they rose to go inside.

It was an older beautiful house. Red brick with black faux shutters at the windows. A Boston fern hung from the porch awning and the hedges lined up against the front of the house were trimmed perfectly. To Dakota it was a southern jewel. As they started into the house Dakota spoke.

"I had no idea it would be this lovely," she said. "I think I should have asked how much the rent is before coming to see it. I am not sure I can afford something this nice on my own."

"That is why I questioned you about your income at your new job," Mrs. Stone replied. "But I am the one who decides how much I charge for rent, and I think you can afford it." The woman continued into the house and Dakota was delighted to see it was furnished.

"You see," Mrs. Stone continued, "this was my mother's home. I don't think I could bring myself to sell it, but I don't want it to go unused. My children loved coming here and I think your children will too. The school is between here and the restaurant you work at, so it will be convenient for you."

Dakota looked around taking in every detail. There was a living room, kitchen, three bedrooms and a bath. The rooms were spacious and there was plenty of closet space. "I love the colors," Dakota told her. "So how much?" Mrs. Stone quoted her a surprisingly low amount and Dakota was glad.

"But I saved the best for last," the woman told her. "Come look." Dakota had not looked at the back yard. As they went out the back door Dakota gasped. There was a wooden deck that led right to the edge of a swimming pool. It was an above ground pool but a nice one and large.

Mrs. Stone saw how pleased Dakota was. "This was for my children when they visited. We just put the cover on. It's too cool for it right now, but this summer your children will enjoy it."

"Oh, you are so right," Dakota replied. "They will absolutely love it!"

Dakota tried to love everything about the place, but all she really wanted was to put the chore behind her. Dakota could not find real joy in anything anymore.

That evening Dakota sat the children down to talk to them. She dreaded telling them they were moving and had put it off far too long. George was at work so at least there would not be a big argument in front of them.

Adam was young. He was sad but he took it well and was ready to go back to his playing. Shane on the other hand had a deer in the headlights look as he asked, "Will we ever see Daddy again? Will we get to finish building our fort? What about our stuff? How will the bus driver know where to pick us up? I don't want to leave!"

Dakota answered all his questions calmly and steadily while on the inside she was screaming, *Why do I have to put my children through this?*

She remembered the swimming pool and told Shane about it. She could see he was still upset but the news of the pool seemed to dull the edges a bit.

Dakota started packing but decided she would let the news set in before actually moving. Besides, moving a small amount of their things at a time would be easier for her too. So for the next few days Dakota took things to her new home before going to work. She was still depressed but did a good job of hiding it and struggled to smile through her work shift.

Finally the day came for moving into their new home. It was Sunday and the children were not happy. They wanted to stay where they were familiar with their surroundings. Adam told Dakota to go ahead without him. "Daddy needs one of us with him," he said.

This child is wise beyond his years, she thought.

"You have to go with me for now," Dakota told him. "You can come back on Friday after school and stay with Daddy for the whole weekend."

Dakota wished things were different but did the best she could and eventually a routine was established and the boys adjusted after awhile. Then, Shane got sick. He had always had problems with allergies and now he cried with an earache.

Dakota called work and school and then called the pediatrician. "Yes," the receptionist said. "With his history you should come on to the office and we will work him in." Just as Dakota suspected he had yet another ear infection.

Since Dakota moved into her own place she was finding out how expensive everything was. Learning how to budget for rent, food, insurance, phone bill, power bill and expenses for the children was a task she had not planned for. The doctor's visit was something else she had not expected and she was almost broke. George had given her a small amount of money as was court ordered but she was living from paycheck to paycheck. The doctor's office agreed to turn the bill over to insurance and bill her later for the difference.

"Okay, Buddy. Let's go get your brother and get you home." When she got the boys settled she did what she did not want to do. She called George. It was thirty minutes before he would be leaving for work. Dakota held her breath as the phone rang for the third time. *Be home,* she thought.

"Hello?"

"Hi, George. I hate to bother you but I knew you would want to know that Shane is sick."

"What's wrong with him?" George asked.

"Allergies and another ear infection." she replied.

"You keeping him at home?"

"Yes," she said. "But he needs antibiotics. The doctor saw him a little while ago."

"So go get him what he needs," George told her.

"I want to," said Dakota, "but I don't have the money. I was hoping you could help me with that."

"You should have thought about that before you moved out. I don't have to give you anything above what the court order says."

"George," Dakota said, "I am not asking you for money to put gas in the car. I am asking for medicine for Shane."

"You'll have to take care of it," George told her.

Dakota was stunned. "Ok, George. I will."

Therefore I say unto you, Take no thought for your life, what ye shall eat, or what ye shall drink; nor yet for your body, what ye shall put on. Is not the life more than meat, and the body than raiment?
Matthew 6:25

CHAPTER SEVEN

Just as Dakota slammed the phone down there was a knock at the door. It was Phyllis from work. Phyllis was younger than Dakota by a few years. She was shorter, slimmer, and prettier. Her blond hair always looked perfect and Dakota admired her. She was loving making new friends at her job. Another friend was a lady named Jackie. Jackie was married, overweight, bossy and had six children. Dakota admired her for completely different reasons.

"Thought you could use these since you have a sick kid in the house." Phyllis said. It was a bag of burgers and fries.

"Thanks, friend. The boys will be thrilled. Phyllis...." Dakota thought for a moment. "Could I ask a huge favor?"

"Ask away," Phyllis replied.

"I need to run an errand. Would you watch the boys? I shouldn't be gone very long."

"Any board games in the house?" Phyllis asked.

"How about Old Maid and Fish instead?" Dakota opened a drawer and pulled out the card games.

"See you later!" Phyllis went through the house calling the boys' names.

As Dakota pulled out of the driveway she was picturing in her mind where she had seen the pawn shop in her new neighborhood. She found it easily and sitting in the parking lot rested her forehead on the steering wheel. She had never been in a pawn shop before. *It will be ok,* she thought. *Just take a deep breath and do it.*

She entered the building and the clang of the bell on the door announced her entrance. Straight ahead of her was the counter and the man behind it smiled as he asked if he could help her find anything.

"Well, I am not here to buy anything," she responded. As Dakota walked toward the counter she removed her wedding band. She laid it on the counter and looked at the man expectantly.

He looked back at her. "Do you want to sell this or pawn it?" he asked.

"Sell," she said. Dakota was surprised at how easily the word rolled off her tongue.

"Are you sure?" The man sounded genuinely concerned.

"I am sure." Dakota watched as he examined and weighed the ring.

"Forty five dollars," he told her.

"Deal," she replied. The man filled out a short form and asked Dakota to sign it. *Well that was easier than I thought it would be.*

Dakota left the pawn shop and headed straight for the pharmacy to get Shane's medicine. Then she went home to cry.

Dakota was learning to manage her money and her time and how to live on her own. It was not easy for her because she had never had to. She had been a tough street kid learning how to survive in dangerous situations, but the years had made her soft. Mother had taught her how to be a lady. She always went to Mother or her mother-in-law to ask for advice and now Mother was gone and she didn't feel comfortable going to George's mother because Granny did not want Dakota to leave her son.

Time was passing quickly. Dakota rose early and went to bed late. Taking care of the boys, taking care of work and taking care of the house was something Dakota was ready to do, but it was long hours and also stressful. There was never enough money but the one thing Dakota splurged on for herself was a pint of vodka. On the weekends the boys spent with their dad, her joy was drinking the whole bottle on Saturday night and sleeping it off on Sunday.

Monday morning Dakota went in to work to find that Mrs. Sheeler was leaving for the day and leaving Dakota in charge of the morning shift. She was a little nervous about being in charge but everything ran smoothly. Near the end of the breakfast shift, Dakota went into the dining room to greet customers. She approached a table with an elderly couple.

"Good morning!" She smiled at them and stopped to chat. "I hope everything was to your satisfaction today." The woman wiped her mouth with a paper napkin and smiled at Dakota.

"It was all delicious." The woman stretched to look at Dakota's name tag.

"Oh, I apologize," she told her. "My name is Dakota. I am a new member of management."

"Yes," the man said. "We knew you were new here. We eat here almost every day."

"Then you will be like family!" Dakota told him. "Would you tell me your names? I will look forward to seeing you."

"I am Pete Andrews and this is my wife of forty-two years, Thelma."

Dakota extended her hand. "So nice to meet both of you."

Just then Dakota felt a curtain of sadness cover her as she walked away from their table. *It takes a special kind of love to last forty-two years,* she thought. *The kind of love Mother and Big Daddy had. They were together fifty-two years.*

That night, Dakota went in to tuck the boys into bed. "Hurry up, Shane. You have been in that bathroom for almost an hour. What are you doing?"

"He's playing diver in the tub," Adam snitched.

"Well let's get you in bed," Dakota said.

"Mom, why are you always sad?"

"What do you mean, Adam?"

Adam stopped fidgeting and looked at his Mother. "You never smile anymore," he told her. "You used to tickle us at bedtime. But you just don't anymore."

Mama's just tired baby," Dakota told him. *It's the truth,* she thought. *Depression will wear you out.*

"Come on, boys. You are going to be late for school!" They had overslept and Dakota had to take them to school on her way to work.

"Why can't we ride the bus like we used to?" asked Shane.

"Yeah," Adam piped in. "I miss Teresa."

"Who is Teresa?" Dakota asked.

"You know," said Adam. "The lady that let me sit on her lap."

"Lady? Oh, you mean the senior in high school. Yeah, that was nice of her. I asked her if she was an angel watching over you."

Adam giggled. "She is not an angel Mom. She didn't have wings."

"Well if you guys don't get in the car I am going to have to grow wings myself to get you to school on time. Adam, don't forget you have a Cub Scout meeting after school. I will bring your shirt, hat and kerchief when I pick you up."

That afternoon Dakota delivered Adam to the scout hut at the church. "Mom, Mr. Jim is waving at you. I think he wants to talk to you."

Dakota spoke to Shane as she was getting out of the car. "Shane, you can get out for a minute to play with the boys if you like. I will call you when I am ready to go."

"Hi, Jim."

"Hi, Dakota. I just wanted to tell you how proud we are that Adam has finished his God and Country program. I ordered the badge and you will get to pin it on him in two weeks. We are having a special ceremony for several of the scouts on that Sunday in church. I wanted to let you know how important it is that he be here, as he is the youngest scout ever to earn that badge in the history of this county!"

"Really?" Dakota looked over at Adam. "He didn't tell me. But of course I am extremely proud of both my boys. Thank you for letting me know early."

"Here is the pin," Jim told her, pushing a box into her hand. "It was only fifteen dollars. But you don't have to pay for it today. You can bring the money to church when you pin it on him."

"Thanks," was all Dakota could say. Then, "Shane, get in the car."

"Why don't you let Shane stay and toss the ball around with some of the boys while I go over a few things with Adam?" Jim asked.

"Oh, okay," agreed Dakota.

The location of the scout hut was closer to the old abandoned chapel than it was to home so Dakota decided to go there and wait for the time to pick the boys up. She was mulling over in her mind how she was going to get the fifteen dollars for the badge. *I'll figure something out,* she thought.

She sat down at the foot of the grave with the broken winged angel when she arrived at the old chapel. *Funny how I spend more time at your grave than I do Mother's. She is so far away, but I can think about her sitting here. Not so sure it helps though. I think it makes me miss her more. Your stone says you were a mother. I guess your children were heartbroken too. I don't think anyone could be as heartbroken as I am at this moment.. About so many things. Daddy, Mother, George, even the friendship of George's mother. I have lost my home and my boys are missing their home and their daddy and I can't even talk to God any more. Even Adam noticed how sad I feel. Those poor babies would be better off without me. Life is just too hard. What a mess I have made out of mine!*

Dakota had seen a lot of heartache in her life, but never had she felt such sadness or gloom as she did today. She was worn down from trying to hide it from everyone and now her sadness was so deep it was beyond tears. All she could do was sit and stare for awhile before getting back in her car to pick the children up.

The week continued on and with every day Dakota's sadness deepened. Twice more she overslept making all of them late for school and work. She was not eating and Jackie and Phyllis noticed. Sitting at break they said so.

"You are losing a lot of weight Dakota. What's your secret?" Jackie asked.

"Whatever it is it can't be good," Phyllis remarked. "Because along with the weight loss has come dark circles under her eyes." Dakota frowned at Phyllis.

"Life is just hard sometimes. That's all," Dakota told them.

Pete and Thelma overheard their conversation. "Life is hard, Dakota. But put your trust in God and He will help you with it." Thelma smiled at her.

Dakota stood and excused herself going back to work.

Many sorrows shall be to the wicked: but he that trusteth in the LORD, mercy shall compass him about. **Psalms 32:10**

CHAPTER EIGHT

"Mom. Mom!" Dakota slowly opened her eyes. It was Friday afternoon. She sat down as soon as she and the children got home and quickly fell asleep. Now she sat up with a sinking feeling in the pit of her stomach. Something was wrong.

"What is it?" she asked Shane.

"We are supposed to go to Dad's," he responded.

Panic set in. Dakota jumped up to look at the time. *Whew! I still have a few minutes.* She opened a can of O-shaped spaghetti and told the boys to eat, then went about packing a bag for them to stay at their Dad's for the weekend. As they were getting ready to go out the door Shane said, "Wait a minute, Mama." He ran into the bedroom with Adam and a couple of minutes later came back.

Both the boys had their hands behind their back and big grins on their faces. "What are you two up to?" she asked.

Shane pulled his hand around to show her what he was holding. "Ta-da!" The sweet smile on his face said so much to her. He was holding a coffee cup he had painted at school. *Happy Mother's Day Best Mom In The World.* He was so proud. That is when Dakota realized Sunday would be Mother's Day and the children would be at their Dad's.

Tears filled Dakota's eyes. "Don't you like it, Mama?" Shane asked her.

"Of course I do!" she told him. "These are happy tears," she said.

Not to be outdone Adam did his Ta-da and gave her a card made out of construction paper. Dakota hugged the boys to her. "I love you guys so much!" she said. "Now, to the car."

I should have expected this, she thought. *Why can't just one thing go right for a change?* A thunderstorm hit just as they went out the door. The crack of lightning was close and the immediate boom of the thunder made her jump. Fat, cold raindrops were blowing sideways and Dakota and the boys were soaked before they reached the car. *Just another day of wishing there were no more days.*

The rain was coming down in sheets and visibility was nonexistent so Dakota drove slowly. Reaching the house Dakota spoke to Shane. "Ask your dad to come to the garage. I need to ask him something." She gave them hugs and sent them inside the house.

George opened the door that led from the house to the garage. He looked at Dakota and said, "You're late!"

"It is raining buckets out there George."

"What do you want?"

"I wanted to ask you since it is Mother's Day on Sunday if I could get the boys back on Sunday morning."

"No," George told her. "It is my weekend to have them and I have made plans to go to my mother's." With that he closed the door.

Dakota cried all the way home. *I feel like I did when I was a little girl,* she thought. *I just want to run away from the pain, but there is no where to run to. Everywhere I go the pain goes with me. It seems no matter what I do I cannot be happy. I want to sleep. I want to die!*

Dakota made it home through the rain and through the tears and went straight to the trunk of her car. She took the vodka into the house and turned the radio on. *Guess it is time for a pity party,* she thought. Then she drank herself to sleep.

Saturday morning Dakota dragged herself to work. *I only have to work a half day today,* she thought. *Then I will do what I have to do.* A plan was forming in Dakota's mind. A plan so vile she dared not think the name of it. She had already set her plan to action. Going into the dining room she looked around for Pete and Thelma. She had become fond of them over the past few weeks. Finding the sweet couple she went to their table to say hello. "Sit with us for a minute," Thelma said.

Accepting her invitation Dakota said to the woman, "I hoped I would see you today. I was going through some of my mother's things last night and found this." She pulled a cameo pin from her pocket and placed it in the woman's hands. "I never wear pins," she told her. "But I hate to see it stay in a closet. It should be worn. I want you to have it."

"Oh, Dakota. This is beautiful. Are you sure you don't want to keep it? I mean after all, it was your mother's."

"I'm sure," she told her. "If you knew my mother you would know that it's okay for you to wear it."

Later, about mid-shift Dakota went to Jackie and whispered. "I am going through some of my stuff and I have a huge bag of clothes I think will fit your oldest daughter. Okay if I bring them to your house this afternoon?"

"Oh, she would love that," Jackie replied.

Finally at break time, Phyllis sat down with Dakota to drink a cup of coffee. Phyllis looked at the diamond teardrop necklace Dakota was wearing. "What a beautiful necklace that is. Kind of fancy for work isn't it?"

"Aw, it's okay," Dakota said. She unclasped the necklace and handed it to Phyllis. "Here, try it on."

Phyllis put the pendant around her neck and pretended to model it. Then she tried to hand it back to Dakota. "No," Dakota said. You keep it."

"What?" Phyllis asked. "No way! Take your necklace."

"I am serious, Phyllis. You always do so much for me. Let me give you this."

"But that looks like a real diamond," said Phyllis.

"It's not worth much," Dakota told her. "It looks better on you anyway!"

Finally her shift was over and Dakota went home to an empty house.

I need to check every room to see if there is anything else I should take to Jackie, she thought. *With six kids I am sure she could use all the help she can get. I should probably take her the hamburger meat I bought for the cookout too so it won't spoil in the fridge.*

Now that Dakota had made up her mind that she didn't want to live it was as though a burden had been lifted. She was energized to get to the point of falling asleep and escaping all the pain this world had to offer. She had convinced herself and was mistakenly believing she would fall asleep and that would be the end of it.

I will do the things I need to do today. Tomorrow I will rest forever.

Dakota gathered everything for Jackie and set it by the front door. Then she went through the whole house to see that it was straightened and in order. She was surprised at how calmly she tackled each task. Even in the boys room she was automated. She placed Mother's Bible, her own Bible and a picture on the boys' bed. Only once did a lump begin to form in her throat and she immediately put it in check thinking only of the relief to come.

Arriving at Jackie's home, she was greeted at the door by six garrulous children. Squeals from every side as she presented something for each of them. Jackie fussed saying how Dakota was spoiling them. Then she sat to have dinner with them before saying she had to run some errands. She tried not to think this would be the last time she saw their grinning faces. Six hugs later, she was on her way.

Dakota drove the thirty miles to Mother and Daddy's grave site. She had spent much time here talking to them and missing them. Today she walked warily across the cemetery to where their stone sat. Sitting cross legged in the center of their resting place she opened her mouth to speak, but nothing came out.

I don't know what to say, Dakota thought. *I want to say so much to you. I miss you. I love you. I need to talk to you about so many things. I haven't seen Junior in awhile, Daddy, he is working and dating and I pretty much leave him alone. He is going to be mad at me tomorrow though. Things have been so bad since you left. Tomorrow is Mother's Day, Mother. So Happy Mother's Day. Before you left, even during the times we didn't talk every day, I knew you were there. I knew I could pick up the phone and you would tell me exactly what I needed to hear or what I needed to do. I never thought about a life where you would not be in it. I don't know how to do it. I don't want to do it. I can't take the hurt, the feeling of being lost, the wandering through each day like a blind person. Every day is too sad to exist.*

Dakota went back to her car. She was amazed that she was not crying. She had brought a sleeve of saltine crackers to feed the ducks in the pond next to Mother and Big Daddy's grave. She retrieved them from the passenger seat. Sitting on the bank throwing the crackers out for the ducks was the most peace she had felt in awhile.

She remembered doing this when she was fourteen years old. She had ridden her bicycle here to look at old graves and especially to feed the ducks. That was so long ago, yet it seemed like yesterday. It never occurred to her that she would be here one day visiting Mother and Daddy's grave.

Finally she drove to get a bottle of vodka and headed back home.

Dakota had just gotten her antidepressant prescriptions filled. All three of them. She still had a few pills leftover from the first round and now she put all of the pills in one bottle. She put the bottle with her car keys on a small table next to the front door. Even in her drunken state she knew she did not want to die at home. She did not want the boys to find her there. Now it occurred to her where she would die. She would go to the Forgotten Chapel. The angel in the cemetery would keep her company.

Be not over much wicked, neither be you foolish: why should you die before your time? Ecclesiastes 7:17

CHAPTER NINE

When Dakota awoke the sun was shining brightly through the living room window. She had fallen asleep there with the TV blaring. She sat up noticing the pounding in her temples and groaned at the taste in her mouth. Standing to stumble into the kitchen she ignored the bottle crashing to the hardwood floor and went to pour a glass of orange juice. Glancing at the clock on the kitchen wall she saw it was after eight and chuckled at having woken up so early. *Guess I knew I had things to do today.*

Dakota drank the juice then rinsed the glass and filled it with water. *May as well get started.* Returning to the living room she opened the medicine bottle and looked at the pills inside. She took three of them out and washed them down. She knew it would take awhile for the medicine to start making her feel like a zombie, so she didn't think about driving after taking them.

Sadness overwhelmed her. Tears unexpectedly slid from her eyes and she wiped them away quickly. *We will have none of that,* she thought. *That is a sign of weakness and I will not be weak today!*

She decided to give the house one more walk through to make sure everything was in order. She took a piece of stationary and wrote a quick note to put in her purse. *I can't do this anymore* was all it said. As she glanced in her bedroom her eye caught sight of the small hinged box holding the God and Country award pin Adam was to receive in a week. She stepped in to pick it up and thought, *Oh no! My baby's pin. He worked so hard for this. He has to get this next week. No one will even think about it. I'll take it to Jim. He will see that Adam gets it.*

Returning to the bottle of pills Dakota was not feeling the effects of the first three so she downed four more. She filled her glass with water, grabbed Adam's pin, her keys and the pills and didn't bother to lock the door behind her.

Settling into the driver's seat, she swallowed several more Xanax. When she started the car she turned the radio to a rock and roll station and turned the volume up. She drove toward the scout leader's house before heading to the abandoned chapel. On the ride there she continued to swallow pill after pill. She was afraid if she didn't she would fall asleep before she had taken enough of them.

When she reached Jim's house she rang the doorbell with Adam's award in her hand. The scout master's wife answered the door and Dakota explained to her that she would not be able to attend the award ceremony next week. "Would you ask Jim to take care of the award for him?" she asked as she extended the box toward her. "He really deserves this."

The woman assured Dakota they would take care of it and Dakota left. As she pulled out of the driveway Dakota reached for two more pills and knocked the bottle over spilling them onto the console. *Well why didn't I think of that? Makes it so much easier to get to them.*

The world began to spin. Dakota was starting to feel dizzy. She took the glass of water from the cup holder and realized the glass was empty. *I didn't even bring any money with me. I can't stop to buy a drink!* Her mind was being covered with cobwebs now and she began to panic. Thankfully, because it was Sunday there was not much traffic this early, so she slowed down.

The restaurant Dakota worked at was nearby. *I can get a free water there,* she thought. *Then I can go to the chapel. It is just a short distance from there.* So she pulled into the parking lot. Getting out of the car she stopped to steady herself. *Whoa, that stuff hits you fast when you stand up!* She was starting to notice things were moving that shouldn't. She yawned and yearned to lie down.

I think I had better hurry. Starting to feel drunk.

After a few seconds Dakota walked into the restaurant. Going up to the counter she told one of the part time cashiers she needed a cup of water. *Oh, I hope she hurries. I don't need to see Mrs. Sheeler. I need to go sit down. I need to get to the chapel.*

Dakota took the cup of water without so much as a thank you and headed back out of the dining room. As she neared the exit someone reached out and grabbed her wrist stopping her in her tracks. It was Pete. Thelma was with him.

"Where are you headed in such a hurry?" he asked her.

Dakota's speech was slurred and loud. "Straight to hell," she responded. Then she pulled away from him and continued on her way. Before she could get out of the door a teenaged girl jumped up from her booth and ran out to the parking lot in front of her. It was Teresa, Adam's bus angel!

Teresa ran to Dakota's car. She pulled the keys from the ignition and noticed the few pills spilled over in the console.

Before Dakota could get to the car she sat down on the asphalt with a smack. Then she blacked out.

When Dakota awoke she could barely make out the face looking back at her. She heard a siren. It sounded like an ambulance a long way off, but in fact Dakota was riding in the back of it. A man was applying pressure to a cut on her head that happened when she passed out in the parking lot. She began to fight the man looking down at her. "I can't breathe, I can't breathe!" she mumbled. She fought to sit up and to breathe in. The paramedic put a mask over her face and as the oxygen was delivered she fell into sleep again.

The next time Dakota awoke she was too weak to fight. A tube was in her nose and her throat and a machine was making loud thumping noises next to her. She opened her eyes in a wild attempt to get someone to notice she was awake but too weak to move her arms. Her mind was screaming for someone to remove the tube. Breathing was difficult at best and she felt like she was drowning. *Please turn that thing off. Just leave me alone. Just let me sleep.* Then, she was out again.

Dakota woke up a few more times in a dream-like state. She was not sure where she was. She couldn't open her eyes but drifted in and out on a cloud. Once she thought she heard Jackie's voice. Another time she thought she saw George carrying a briefcase. Yet again she felt a moving sensation as though she were riding in a car. Finally, she slept. For three days.

"Well, hello sleepyhead." The woman reached out and picked up Dakota's hand. She began checking her pulse and looking at her watch. Dakota tried to move her stiff body.

"How long have I been asleep?" Dakota asked. She did not recognize her own voice because of the hoarseness.

"Oh, about thirty-six hours now," the nurse told her.

"What? That long?"

"That's what happens when you swallow eighty-three pills."

"Eighty-three? How do you know I swallowed eighty three?"

"Well, that's how many they extracted from you. Don't know how many dissolved to make you sleep so long," the nurse said.

"Guess I didn't swallow enough of them, huh? Where am I?"

"You're in the hospital. Now that you are awake a doctor will be in to see you shortly." The nurse wrote something on a clipboard and started for the door.

"I won't need a doctor," Dakota said. "If you will un-hook this IV I'll call for a ride home."

"Sorry," said the nurse. "I don't think you understand. This is not a regular hospital Sweetie. You were transferred here from your local hospital. This is where we do mental evaluations. We couldn't let you go home if we wanted to. Let me call the doctor so he can explain it to you."

Well of all things to mess up. Dakota was so mad at herself and now the doctor came in to confirm what the nurse had already told her.

"Suicidal patients are required by law to have thirty days evaluation and treatment...minimum. We can't let you leave. You signed insurance forms stating you agreed to treatment anyway, with the stipulation you would stay for thirty days or the shortest amount of time allowed by your insurance, which is usually thirty days."

"What? What do you mean I signed?"

"Don't you remember?" the doctor asked her.

"No. I don't," she replied.

"Well that is not surprising. Blacking in and out of consciousness the memories rarely stay." The doctor studied Dakota's face for a moment. "We want to help you to get your depression under control, Mrs. Day. We would like to show you that life can be valuable. Here is a preview of what you can expect."

Dakota stared ahead at nothing in particular hardly hearing what the physician was saying. "You will be given a thorough physical examination, you will be given a mental evaluation and depending on those results we will then determine a plan of action for getting you on the right track."

Wonder how many times he had to practice that little speech.

"Do you understand what I just told you?" the doctor asked.

"Yes."

"Would you like to get up for awhile?"

"No thanks."

"I won't insist for now. But you must get up to take a shower this afternoon."

"What if I prefer to stay in bed?" Dakota was angry and wanted the world to leave her alone.

"Then unfortunately someone else will have to give you a shower." The doctor stood and left the room.

The same nurse Dakota saw when she woke up was standing in the doorway. "He don't play," she said. "Let me know when you are ready for that shower."

The nurse's name was Amy. She was fresh out of nursing school and determined to be the best nurse since Florence Nightingale. She seemed to be in tune with the need of every patient and smiled through every task. Her five-foot six-inch frame was slim. Dakota tried to think of the color of the girls hair that was pulled back into a tidy ponytail at her neck and all she could compare it to was black licorice. Her eyes were the same color.

"Okay, Amy," Dakota told her. "Let's get the shower over with." Amy removed the IV and stayed with Dakota until she was sure Dakota was steady on her feet then left her to her task. When Dakota entered the room again she saw a toothbrush and hairbrush on the bed. *Guess if I don't brush my teeth they will have someone else do that too.* After taking care of her personal grooming she crawled back into bed. She was tiring quickly. She wasn't sure if it was because she had slept so long or because she was so depressed. Amy came back into the room. "Feeling better?" she asked.

"I need a razor to shave my legs," Dakota told her.

Amy didn't miss a beat. She went about fluffing the pillows and tightening the sheets. "No razors, no belts, no shoe strings, no pills, etcetera, etcetera." She stopped moving and talking and patted Dakota's hand. "Just relax for awhile and try to think about something that makes you smile.

And in those days shall men seek death, and shall not find it; and shall desire to die, and death shall flee from them. Revelation 9:6

CHAPTER TEN

The next morning Dakota awoke with Amy making noises with her breakfast tray. "Ugh, what is that smell?" Dakota asked her.

"It is scrambled eggs," Amy said. "Your stomach is going to be very picky about what it will keep down today. The IV was your friend for three days, but it is time for you to slowly introduce food again. Starting with eggs."

"I'd rather sleep," Dakota responded.

"Nope! Up and at 'em!"

Why does this girl remind me of Snow White? Sweet, cute, helpful, yet bossy and demanding!

Dakota picked up the fork and scooped up a bite of eggs. Some fell off the fork bouncing across the plate. "If I am going to be tortured while I am here could we use some other means?"

Amy smiled. "They are cold because you ignored them for so long. Eat!"

Dakota forced herself to eat half the eggs and sipped the warm coffee. "Don't suppose you could slip in a spike of vodka for the coffee?"

"The doctor will be making rounds shortly," she said. "Maybe you can talk him into it." She winked at Dakota and left the room.

Dakota had fallen back to sleep. It was all she wanted to do now. She heard a knock at the door. "Come in," she muttered expecting to see the doctor. She was surprised to see the preacher standing there just inside the door. "Come on in," she told him. He didn't move an inch. She sat up in bed and using both hands attempted to smooth her hair.

"Someone put your name on the prayer request list," he told her. "Mind if I say a prayer?"

"Of course I don't mind."

Dakota stared incredulously at the preacher. He had barely entered the room and when he began to pray he stood in the same place as though Dakota might have a disease that was contagious. Dakota had many engaging conversations with this man in the past. Now, he was formal, rigid, a stranger, and an uncomfortable one at that.

After his short, awkward prayer he bade her goodbye with, "Take care."

Dakota just shook her head and slid back down under the warm blankets. *Good thing I didn't really need prayer,* she thought.

That afternoon the doctor came in to expand on a course of action for Dakota's treatments. He handed her a sheet of paper.

"You will have a structured schedule for most of the day," he told her. "All of your meals beginning tomorrow will be in the dining room. You can see the times on that paper. Don't be late if you want to eat. That paper also has the classes you will be attending and the highlighted ones are the times you will attend."

The doctor cleared his throat and looked at his copy of the schedule as though he too were trying to figure it out.

"It can be a bit confusing," he said. "But you'll get the hang of it. For instance there are three craft classes. You just go to the one at the highlighted time in the highlighted room number."

Dakota said facetiously, "Sounds like highlighted summer camp."

"You will be kept busy. You will be administered medication throughout the day. You will go to counseling sessions. As you can see on your schedule dinner is at five. The agenda doesn't show anything after five, but here is what you can expect. Visiting hours are from six o'clock to eight. Visitors are not allowed in your room. Visiting is in the two common areas only. If you do not have visitors you can sit in the common area to watch TV or read or talk to other patients. You can go to your room after eight. Lights out is at ten o'clock."

"Can I just come back to my room after dinner?" Dakota interrupted.

"No." His answer was quick and adamant.

"Doc, I don't see how I can possibly do all this. My body is so tired. My mind is exhausted. All I want to do is sleep twenty-four seven."

"I am prescribing new meds for you. These medicines will get you going again. You will report to the meds window at the times written on your schedule. You will be given water and expected to swallow all meds in front of the nurse."

Great.

"What kind of meds?" Dakota inquired. "The kind that zone me out?"

"We will try different treatments until we find what is best for you," he replied. "You'll be asked at the end of the day about how the day went. You'll be asked if the medicines agreed with you."

"How many prescriptions this time?" she asked him. "I was on three before. But I didn't really take them all the time. I had to work and they made me feel stupid."

The doctor chuckled at that. "I am starting you out on three again and since you don't like the hospital food I am giving you a steroid to improve your appetite too. If you look at mid-day schedule you will see that you have a gym class that is imperative. We will talk about how these medicines, exercise and counseling are working after you have been here for about a week." He patted Dakota on the shoulder and said, "Good luck with those craft classes!"

Dakota rolled her eyes and grimaced.

Dakota donned the only outfit she had and unwillingly left her room. She approached the closest common room like a cat on the prowl. She was skittish and had no idea what to expect. She had never set foot in a mental hospital before.

The room was brightly lit. The walls were painted sage green and several paintings brought to mind warm comfortable places through beach scenes. There were cushy oversized chairs and chaise with an assortment of magazines on tables.

Dakota sat in one of the chairs and looked at the itinerary the doctor had given her. As she studied it a voice spoke from behind her.

"You'll have it memorized in a couple of days," the woman said.

Dakota looked up as the stranger walked around to sit across from her.

"Hi," the woman said.

"Hi," Dakota responded.

"You are probably wondering the same thing I am so let's get it out there. My name is Cotton and I'm here because I don't want to live. Your turn."

"Cotton? Is that your last name?" Dakota asked.

"No. It's a nickname. Your turn."

"I'm Dakota and I'm here for the same reason."

Dakota was drawn to the woman. She was an interesting character. Cotton was a slight figure but outgoing. She wore a cheap housecoat with oversized pockets and had a limp when she walked.

"Can I see your schedule?" Cotton asked.

"Sure." Dakota handed it to her.

Dakota studied the woman's wrinkled face through squinting eyes. *I'll bet she is younger than she looks,* she thought. *You can tell just by looking at her she has lived a hard life. Her blue eyes would be beautiful if they weren't so washed out and faded and her hair is so thin she must have lost a lot of it. Probably to meds.*

"Okay," Cotton said. "Looks like we have almost the same schedule except that while you are at gym, I will be getting shock treatments."

Dakota's eyes widened and her eyebrows shot up. "Shock treatments?"

"Yeah. They send electricity through my brain trying to change the chemistry."

Dakota was horrified. She had heard terrible stories about shock treatments. "Does it hurt?" she asked.

"Nope. They put me under first and I don't feel a thing. It is an experimental thing for me. They are still trying to figure out what is wrong with me. I could tell them but I think they should earn their money. Don't you?" Then the woman smiled a huge smile.

"Come on," Cotton said. "You might as well get the grand tour. I will show you where all the classes and counseling takes place then we will check out the dining room and gym. They are located next to each other. But first we have to report for meds."

The two went to a small window near the hall where the private rooms were located. A nurse sitting behind the glass asked them in turn to say their full name and birth date. She then passed a small cup of water and a cup holding their medicine through a hole in the window. Both women put the pills in their mouths then turned up the water. After walking away from the nurse Cotton turned a corner and spit the pills into her hand.

"What are you doing?" Dakota was incredulous.

"Shhhhh!" Cotton pressed an index finger against her lips and taking Dakota by the arm pulled her farther along into another hallway. "You can't tell," she said as she pushed the pills into her pocket. "Pinky Promise."

Okay. What is this person...twelve?

"But you will not get well if you don't swallow your medicine."

"Really?" Cotton looked at Dakota hard. "This coming from someone else who wants to die?"

"How did you do that?" Dakota asked her.

"It's easy. You simply put the pills under your tongue and let the water slide down without them. You thinking about doing it too?"

Dakota didn't say anything but walked along in deep thought. Cotton showed her all the places she would need to know and then they went into the dining room for breakfast.

As they sat drinking coffee and picking at their food they began to swap life stories. Dakota told all about how she ran away from an abusive mother at the age of eleven and was taken in by foster parents. She told of the hurt of losing them. She bragged about her beautiful children and spoke of her failed marriage.

Cotton in turn told her about her life of drugs and an abusive husband and surprised Dakota with the news that she too had two children. "They are being raised by my mother," she said. "That is not something I am proud of. But they are better off with her."

By the time the two women had to go to a counseling session they had forged a friendship and sat next to each other from that day on in counseling and classes.

As they entered the crafts class Cotton said, "Here. Sit by me. We start a new craft today. We can help each other."

Dakota looked around. There was a handmade ceramic plaque on the wall that said *"Busy Hands Are Happy Hands." How corny,* she thought.

After spending the whole day together, Dakota was glad to have some quiet time to herself while Cotton visited with her mother and her children.

Dakota didn't have any visitors but someone had dropped off a suitcase of clothing. She later found out that Jackie and Phyllis had brought them, but the doctor had decided it was too soon for visitors, so they left disappointed. Dakota was glad. She was not ready to face anyone.

Know ye not that ye are the temple of God, and that the Spirit of God dwelleth in you? 1 Corinthians 3:16

CHAPTER ELEVEN

The next morning Dakota entered the common area to find Cotton waiting for her. They went to get their meds and again when they rounded the corner Cotton spit the pills into her hand. She was not surprised when Dakota followed suit.

"Here's the secret to make this work," Cotton told her. "Let me see your pills." Dakota unfurled her fist to show Cotton the four pills. "Okay. The white pill is fifty milligrams of prednisone. That is the one that peps you up and makes you hungry. Take that one and hide the others."

Dakota quickly popped the small pill into her mouth and swallowed it. Then she shoved the rest deeply into her jeans pocket.

She had taken one round of the pills the day before, so she was beginning to feel hungry. Her throat was now healed from the pumping of her stomach so at breakfast she ate a slice of bacon and limp toast and followed Cotton to a group counseling class.

The leader of the class was called Wanda. She sat in a chair identical to everyone else's, but her feet barely touched the floor. She was middle aged and wrinkling early, and Dakota wondered why on earth someone would want to spend their life listening to a bunch of whining, suicidal, miserable weaklings. Dakota decided for the woman she had enough to deal with without listening to Dakota's sob story; so Dakota just sat and listened without saying a word. Wanda put up with that for two sessions.

"So, Dakota, do you have something you would like to share with us?"

"No thanks." Dakota replied.

"Well we all have our reasons for being here," Wanda told her. "This is your third day in this group. We encourage everyone to share here. If you choose not to we will have to have private sharing sessions. So, do you have anything to say?"

Dakota sat still saying nothing. Wanda moved on to pick on someone else.

After the class Cotton looped her arm into Dakota's as they headed for crafts. "Oh you should have said something in there."

"Why? She will just forget about it. It was not a big deal."

"Boy, do you have a lot to learn," Cotton said. "She will not forget it. Trust me. That lady does not forget anything. Now she will be on your case big time!"

"So long as she does not bother the drinking mug they gave me when I checked in. I keep it by my bedside with the screw cap on and a straw in it. Hopefully the nurse will think there is water in it."

Cotton replied, "What a good idea! Hiding them in plain sight. But if she picks that cup up and hears the pills rattling..."

"She won't," Dakota interrupted her. I wrapped them in napkins."

"Brilliant," Cotton said.

The two entered the common room and sat for a few minutes waiting for the next session. "I have an idea," Cotton told Dakota. "Let's make a pact. Since we are both going to die we can plan it to be at the same time. Let's plan it for the seventeenth. That is one day before I am supposed to go home and two days before you are supposed to go home. If we swallow all the pills at lights out, we will go to sleep and not wake up. That way we don't have to worry about someone finding us that we don't want to find us. What do you think?"

"Well, since I have been in here, George has had the kids and they are much better off with him than with me. I miss them so bad, but I can't do for them like he can. He was a tyrant to me, but not the boys. There has been one time I had visitors here and they were turned away from the door. I doubt they will come back. So yes." Dakota made that decision quickly and was glad to know when she would take that step again.

The women hugged to seal the deal.

The next day Wanda told Dakota to stay in her seat when she dismissed the group counseling session. Cotton leaned over to say, "Told you so." Dakota made a face and slumped down in her chair. Dakota's normal weight was one hundred twenty pounds but she noticed when she slid down her jeans were getting tight. *Think I am going to have to stop taking that little white pill and add it to my collection.*

Wanda began their private sessions which cut into her craft time. She couldn't decide which she hated more.

"I know you were brought here for attempted suicide," Wanda began. "What I need to know is why you wanted to die. Will you share that with me?"

"You don't know me," Dakota said. "Why would you even want to know?"

"Well, I could say because it is my job. But I won't. I want to know because I care about people." Wanda pulled the plastic lunch room chair closer to Dakota scraping it across the tiled floor. I have read your folder, Dakota. There is a lot of history in your medical files. It has your religion listed as Christian. So, you know the Lord?"

Dakota squirmed. "I used to."

Wanda leaned in. "So what happened that you stopped knowing Him?"

Dakota was not comfortable with this stranger getting so deep into her personal life. She thought about answering but decided it was none of Wanda's business, so she stood and left the room. She was so distraught she would have left the hospital except that the doors were locked and could only be opened by personnel. So she went to the common area and picked up a magazine. Pretending to read she tried to ignore Wanda when she followed Dakota out of the smaller room. The woman sat across from her and softly said, "You can't run from Him forever." Then Wanda stood and left Dakota with an empty, lost feeling in her gut.

That evening, Dakota was surprised when the night nurse told her she had visitors. "The front common room is not as crowded if you would like to go in there and we will send them in."

Great. Wonder who it is. I hope no one has told Junior I am here. It would be better if he didn't know. Knowing George, he hasn't told anyone.

As Dakota walked into the room she was immediately pounced upon with a bear hug. It was Jackie. Phyllis followed suit. The three sat on a corner chaise and Jackie babbled on about how they missed her at work and when was she coming back. Pete and Thelma sent well wishes and said a card was on it's way through the mail. Then the mood became somber.

"Why didn't you talk to us?" Phyllis asked.

"Maybe we could have helped," said Jackie. "We knew things were tough for you. Guess we just didn't realize how tough."

"Aw. You guys are so sweet. But there was nothing you could do to change how things were. There was nothing I could do to change it."

"Mrs. Sheeler says hello and she said to tell you that you still have a job if you want it. The customers are asking about you all the time." Jackie took Dakota's hand. "We really miss you."

Dakota felt the unexpected sting of tears. "Oh, wow. Look at that." She looked at the electric clock on the wall. "Visiting time is up!"

"But we just got here," Jackie protested.

"No, no. You have been here thirty minutes and I may get in trouble if I go over my allotted time."

The visitors rose to leave. Dakota hugged them both goodbye and went back to her favorite chair in the other room to try not to think. She looked around the room and spotted two little girls standing in front of where Cotton sat holding a doll. The girls had their mother's blue eyes and both had long blond locks of hair. They were giggling and hugging her. *They are going to miss her,* Dakota thought. *My boys will get used to me being gone. They will be fine. They will be better off.*

"So," Wanda said the next day. "Would you like to share in group today?"

Dakota thought about it. *If I don't she will badger me afterwards, but if I do all these people have the right to ask me anything. Lose, lose situation. Being badgered by one has to be better than being harassed by a room full.* "No thanks."

"Then stay after group," Wanda told her.

Dakota was not looking forward to another private session but did as she was told. After everyone else left Wanda and Dakota sat in silence for a full five minutes. The quiet was starting to get to Dakota. *What is she doing?* Finally Dakota broke the hush. "So, you wanted to talk to me?"

"Yes," Wanda told her. "But I don't want to be the only one talking. I would like to have a conversation with you and I would appreciate it if you would not walk out in the middle of it."

"Okay. I had that coming." Dakota stood and walked to the only window in the room. She looked at a courtyard with an assortment of foliage without even seeing it.

Wanda didn't move but continued to talk. "All I want from you today is...why. We both know you wanted to die. Tell me why."

Dakota took in a deep breath, then exhaled loudly. "You are not going to give up are you?" she asked.

"No, Dakota. I want to help you whether you want it or not. For today just one answer. Why?"

"Why I wanted to die?"

"Yes."

"Well that one is easy," replied Dakota. "Have you ever been in so much pain that no Codeine, no Valium, no Xanax or any kind of street drug or alcohol could kill it? Or if you escaped the pain for awhile the pain was always there when the pills or the liquor wore off? That is why I wanted to die. Because there was no other way to get away from the constant agony."

"What was the pain from?"

"Un-uh," Dakota shook her head no. "You said just one answer. May I go now?"

Wanda did not show her frustration but dismissed Dakota already making a list of questions in her head. *This cookie is a tough one,* she thought.

Let all bitterness and wrath and anger and clamor and slander be put away from you, along with all malice. Ephesians 4:31

CHAPTER TWELVE

"Just a few more hours," was the greeting Dakota received from Cotton. "Think we will have enough?"

"More than enough," Dakota responded. "I'm just ready for it to be done." She was feeling especially low today. She decided she would take the little white pill today so that Wanda or Amy would not question why she was so down and not eating.

"You okay?" asked Cotton.

"I'm fine."

"Wanda is starting to get to you, isn't she?"

"No!" Dakota replied emphatically.

"Yes she is. I can always tell when the counselors are getting to someone. They got to me the last time I was here."

"How many times have you been in here, Cotton?"

"This is my fourth and final time."

"I can't believe they haven't found our pill stash," Dakota told her.

"They aren't looking for it," Cotton replied. "Come on, let's get breakfast then head to crafts."

Dakota was glad the dining room was not crowded this morning. Cotton noticed it too. "Hmmm. They must have sent some people home yesterday."

"So long as they still made plenty of coffee I don't care how many they send home." Dakota filled her cup to the rim. "I think I will skip crafts this morning. Just not into it today."

Cotton raised her eyebrows and asked, "What are you going to do?"

"Probably sit here and sip coffee awhile then walk the halls till time for group."

"You sure you want to do that?" asked Cotton. "What if you get caught?"

"Nobody knows my schedule but you and me."

"Suit yourself. Just don't draw attention to what you are doing. Remember...we fulfill our pact tonight!"

Cotton left for crafts and Dakota sat with her coffee until the last person got up to leave. She then began to walk up and down the corridor where the crafts class was. On her third round she almost ran headlong into Wanda.

"Sorry," Dakota said.

""What are you doing?" Wanda asked.

"Um...just headed to the Ladies Room," Dakota lied.

"Why didn't you just use the one in the crafts room?" Wanda stuck her head in the crafts class and told the teacher that Dakota would be spending the next hour with her.

Great. A whole hour.

Taking the first chair she came to, Dakota sighed loudly and slumped. She expected to hear a lecture. Instead, Wanda looked through some papers on her desk and retrieving a report she turned a chair backwards and sat across from Dakota.

"I now give myself permission to drill you with all the questions I want to. You, of course can get up and leave at any time," Wanda said. "But be forewarned...if you do I have the power to have your guest status extended for another month. It is entirely up to you."

Dakota was shocked into listening. She had no idea they could make her stay longer.

"Now, just for the record," Wanda continued. "At this point in time you are not considered a 'mental' patient. Trying to commit suicide does not mean you are crazy, but don't push your luck. If I decide to we can have you lodging in one of the padded cells with the stroke of an ink pen."

Wanda now had Dakota's attention. A padded cell was the last place she wanted to be at lights out tonight.

"Get comfortable," Wanda told her. "Just answer the questions."

"Think back to your first thought of being so unhappy that you wanted to die. What were the circumstances causing that?"

Dakota thought for a moment but she did not have to think long. "When Mother died."

"Your Dad died too, right?"

"Yes," Dakota said. "A few months before Mother."

"And these were your foster parents?"

"Yes, but they were the best parents anyone could ask for."

Wanda caught Dakota off guard with her next question as she expected another question about Mother and Daddy. "How long have you been mad at God?" Wanda asked.

Dakota shot a startled look at her. "Since Mother died."

"Anything else you have been upset about?"

"Yes."

Wanda took her eyes from the paper to look at Dakota. "Are you really going to make me ask?"

"Leaving my husband," Dakota told her.

"Many people go through these things, Dakota. Granted not all at once. But why would you want to die?"

Dakota was ready to explode. Too many questions. Too many memories. Too much stress. *Just tell her. Tell her what she wants to hear then maybe she will leave you alone.*

"Okay, okay," Dakota said. Then she began her rant as the flood gates opened. "You have no idea how much I depended on my parents. You have no idea how it is to live for years with a husband that wants you as a piece of property instead of a wife. You have no idea of how hard it is to wonder if what you are doing is best for your children. Do you know what it is like to lay awake nights wondering how you are going to make rent?" Dakota swiped at a tear that had unexpectedly escaped.

"Eventually you feel like you just want to die because with every passing day everything just gets worse instead of better. The thoughts drive you to drink because the alcohol dulls the pain. But guess what?" Dakota patted her chest. "When the alcohol wears off, the pain is still there. There is no end to it. Can't you see how hopeless it is? I am trapped in an endless cycle. When I was a child I was trapped in an abusive home. I was able to escape that. But I was the only one I had to worry about. Now I have two boys that depend on me when I can't even depend on myself!" Dakota stood and walked to the window to look at the courtyard.

"Then there are the panic attacks. Heart pounding, breathless, clammy-skinned attacks that pop up out of nowhere taking my breath away, making my chest hurt and wishing I would die so I don't have to keep experiencing the pain."

Dakota stopped to take in a ragged breath. Wanda thought she was through and pushed for one more question.

"So where does God fit into all this, Dakota?"

Dakota collapsed to the floor weeping. *I can't do this,* she thought.

Dakota looked up at Wanda. "May I go to the bathroom to wash my face, please?"

"Go ahead."

When Dakota left the bathroom she went to the common room and sat down. Cotton entered the room. She went over to kneel in front of Dakota. Seeing her red eyes Cotton said, "I knew it. I knew she would get to you."

"Not now, Cotton. Nothing has changed. I just need to breathe."

The two went back to the group room to finish the regular class. Wanda addressed Dakota. *Oh please don't keep doing this,* she thought.

"Dakota, do you have living arrangements when you leave?"

"Yes, I got word my house is just as I left it and I am welcome back there."

"Do you have a job to go to?"

"Yes. My old job is still open to me."

"You are fortunate. Not everyone has those options."

"Yes, Ma'am. Fortunate."

Later that evening, Amy came into the common room to find Dakota. "You have a visitor!"

Dakota thought that it was probably someone from work bringing her a schedule since she was supposed to be released in a couple of days.

"Amy, do you think we could visit in the courtyard? Some fresh air would be nice."

"I will ask," Amy replied.

A few minutes later Amy came back with a key and told Dakota to go into the courtyard. "I will bring your visitor to you."

Dakota sat on a round of bricks forming a flower bed. She looked up just as her visitor came outside. It was Teresa, Adams angel and the teenager that had saved Dakota from the overdose.

Teresa walked over to Dakota and hugged her tight.

"Hello, Mrs. Day."

"Hi, Teresa..."

"I have been wanting to come see you but I couldn't get here 'til now. I have been getting ready to go to Charleston. I am going to college there in the fall."

"Congratulations, Teresa. I am happy for you. I'm glad I got to see you. I wanted to say thank you for everything. For keeping an eye on my children and for...well...you know."

"Mrs. Day, I have been praying for you. You don't have to thank me for anything. It was God watching over you and your children. You should thank Him."

"Yeah, well, God and I have not been speaking much lately."

"Mrs. Day, may I say something?"

"Sure, Teresa. What is it?"

"If you and God are not talking it is not God's fault. The Bible says nothing can separate us from His love. He loves you today just as much as He did on the day you were born."

Dakota felt a pang of guilt. Something stirred in her heart. Teresa continued.

"We all have things happen that make us sad or wonder if anyone cares but no matter what, God cares. And He can help you. But you have to ask Him and you have to trust that He will. Adam told me that you missed your mother too much. Well you will never have to worry about missing God. God will never leave you. He is hurting because you left Him."

Hot tears streamed down Dakota's face.

"Mrs. Day? May I pray for you?"

Dakota grabbed Teresa's hand and bowed her head. When the girl was done praying Dakota told her, "Stay right here. Don't move!"

Dakota ran inside going from room to room searching for Cotton. Finally she found her watching television in the first common room. Kneeling in front of Cotton with tears still streaming she said, "We can't do it. The pact is broken."

"I knew Wanda would get to you," Cotton declared.

"No, Cotton. Wanda did not get to me. I have just realized that I care about you and I won't let you do this. Go get the pills you have saved and bring them to me. If you don't I will have to tell Wanda and Amy. I will go get mine and we will meet back here in exactly one minute."

Both women went into the bathroom and flushed the pills. They went back into the common room and hugged tightly.

Dakota took Cotton by the hand and said, "Come with me. There is someone remarkable that I want you to meet."

And said unto him, Hearest thou what these say? And Jesus saith unto them, Yea; have ye never read, Out of the mouth of babes and sucklings thou hast perfected praise? Matthew 21:16

AUTHOR'S NOTE

Suicide is at an epidemic rate and takes the lives of over 40,000 Americans every year. Suicide is not just a secular disease. Depression can affect Christians too. Sometimes depression is a chemical imbalance. Sometimes it is simply circumstances. Not everyone who gets depressed will attempt suicide but the number of failed attempts is near half a million people yearly. These numbers are just for those in the United States.

Signs of depression are not always obvious. Dakota was able to hide hers most of the time. But if you notice someone with these changes taking place take a closer look. Sudden change in appetite, sleep changes, outbursts of anger, new interest in alcohol or drugs, or self-loathing. Help is available with medication, counseling, exercise, diet and best of all, prayer.

Dakota's situation was due to her own misgivings. When things went amiss she tried to handle them herself and depression set in. Where

Dakota went wrong was putting her trust in another human being, instead of God. She needed a light in the darkness of her world to look to for guidance. She set the flame to follow in Mother when she should have gone to God for everything she needed.

He is one Flame that will never go out.

National Suicide Prevention Lifeline
1 (800) 273-8255

ABOUT THE AUTHOR

Deborah Norton currently resides in a small town in the upstate of South Carolina. A happy and loving mother of three and 'Nana' to many, she is passionate about life and advocates intervention whenever children are neglected or abused.

Made in the USA
Charleston, SC
11 June 2015